# THE HEARTBEAT OF EVANGELISM

## Keeping the Main Thing, the Main Thing

# H. J. Peasley

**AMBASSADOR-EMERALD INTERNATIONAL**
GREENVILLE, SOUTH CAROLINA • BELFAST, NORTHERN IRELAND

***I want to express my thanks to:***

Rev. Victor Maxwell and Dr. Jackie Hughes of Northern Ireland, and Rev. Nico van Wyk, and Mr. Twakkies du Toit of Evangelism Explosion South Africa, for encouraging me to write such a book.

To my co-worker Rev. Errol Wesson, who has been such a fine inspiration and example to me in the area of personal evangelism. Much of the material in this book is what he and I have presented in seminars.

To the memory of the late Rev. Roger Voke of Cape Town, South Africa, who was a mentor to me. His enthusiasm and passion for souls has been a constant challenge and a vibrant memory as I have sought to put this book together.

To my wife Antoinette and our children, especially, because they have always been my best supporters!

To my secretary, Mrs. Bobby Watt, who has spent hours typing and re-typing these notes.

To Dr. Terry McGee, who was willing to take time to edit the manuscript.

But most of all, glory and praise is given to God and His beloved Son the Lord Jesus Christ, my own personal Saviour and Lord. "The love of Christ constraineth me!"

> *Sudden before my inward open vision,*
> *Millions of faces crowd up into view.*
> *Sad eyes that say: "For us is no provision*
> *Give us your Saviour too".*
> *"Give us" they cry "your cup of consolation*
> *Never to our outreaching hands 'tis passed*
> *We long for the desire of every nation,*
> *But oh! We die so fast".*

*The Heartbeat of Evangelism:*
*Keeping the Main Thing, the Main Thing*

*Copyright © 1999 H.J. Peasley*

Published by
**Ambassador-Emerald International**
1 Chick Springs Road, Suite 203
Greenville, SC 29609 USA

and

Ambassador Productions
16 Hillview Avenue
Belfast, Northern Ireland
BT5 6JR

Cover and internal design © 1999 Grand Design
Cover photography © 1999 Photodisc

www.emeraldhouse.com

# Contents

# Introduction

If you had only five minutes with a person before you knew he would die, what would you say to him?

If you, as a preacher, knew that this was the last message that you would be preaching, what would you preach?

If you could give a message to the world this very hour, what would it be?

If someone came back from heaven, what would he say to us?

If someone came back from hell, as the rich man of Luke 16 requested that someone from heaven might return to warn his brothers, what would his message be?

Evangelism, spreading the Gospel—the Good News—is surely the greatest challenge facing the church of Jesus Christ today. Jonathan Edwards said as a prayer: "Lord, stamp eternity on my eye balls."

Another said "You can't take the Gospel to the wrong address."

Another said "There is no discharge from preaching the gospel in time of war."

I trust that this book will cause your heart to be stirred again about the Great Commission.

# Chapter One

# THE MAIN THING

## WHAT? - ITS PLACE

1. DEFINING ITS IMPORTANCE

2. DETERMINING ITS INSCRIPTIONS

    2.1 Its Place in the Scriptures

    2.2 Its Priority in the life of Jesus

    2.3 Its Predominance in the life of Paul

    2.4 Its Practice in the early Church

    2.5 Its Power in Society

3. DESCRIBING ITS IMPLICATIONS

Some time ago I was intrigued to read the following quote by someone: "The main thing is to keep the main thing the main thing." I subsequently saw this being mentioned in various church bulletins, i.e "Keeping the Main Thing—will take place on Thursday night." This caught my attention, so I set out to discover what was meant by the "Main Thing".

In a nutshell, the Main Thing is the attempt to spread the Good News of the Gospel of the Lord Jesus Christ to all mankind. It simply means to evangelize!

For us to understand the subject clearly, let us examine the question under the following headings:

1. DEFINING ITS IMPORTANCE

2. DETERMINING ITS INSCRIPTIONS

3. DESCRIBING ITS IMPLICATIONS

## 1. DEFINING ITS IMPORTANCE

It is possible that many do not see the spreading of the Gospel as the Main Thing for the church today! It may be helpful if we explain what the Main Thing is.

- The Gospel is important because of what it is. It is the Good News.

- The Gospel is important because of Who it is centered in. It is said that Egypt without the Nile is not Egypt; so the Gospel without Jesus is no Gospel.

When Jesus went back to His hometown of Nazareth in Galilee, He went to the synagogue on the Sabbath day "as was His custom". He was invited to read from the Scriptures, and He unravelled the scrolls to the book of Isaiah and read from chapter 61:1. To find that particular place, would apparently have meant unravelling over 30 yards of scroll. He was obviously well versed in the Scriptures and knew exactly what He wanted to share. Luke 4:17 says, "And there was delivered unto Him the book of the prophet Esaias. And when He had opened the book, He found the place where it was written, 'The Spirit of the Lord is upon me, because He hath anointed me to preach the Gospel to the poor, He hath sent me to heal the broken-hearted, to preach deliverance to the captives, and recovering of sight to the blind, to set at liberty them that are bruised, to preach the acceptable year of the Lord'." He then went further in verse 21 and said, "This day is this Scripture fulfilled in your ears." Obviously He was the fulfillment of this Good News.

The Good News was, and is, that Jesus Christ, the Son of God, had come and promised a new life, free from the condemnation of sin and its power. Surely this is the greatest news the world has ever heard, and should be proclaimed from the housetops.

- It's good news about life—in Christ we step from existence to living.

- It's good news about sin—our sin has been conquered at the cross, and we can be free from its penalty.

- It's good news about death—death has lost its sting.

- It's good news about the law—we now live under grace, and the need to strive for peace of mind is removed.

- It's good news about heaven—does not need to be "pie in the sky" but a glorious reality.
- It's good news about the devil—he has been conquered once for all.
- It's good news about God—He is not a God before Whom we must cringe, but He is one who has gone after us in our sin by His love and mercy and made it possible for us to know Him personally through His Son the Lord Jesus Christ.
- This good news is positive and not negative, dynamic and not static, and it is qualitative and not just quantitative.

## 2. DETERMINING ITS INSCRIPTIONS

### 2.1 Its Place in the Scriptures

**It is Emphasized in the Sayings of Jesus:**

Look at His first request: In Matt 4:19, as Jesus commenced His ministry here on earth, the Bible tells us what He said concerning this ministry. Verse 18 says "And Jesus walking by the sea of Galilee, saw two brethren, Simon called Peter, and Andrew his brother, casting a net in the sea; for they were fishers." Verse 19, "He saith unto them, Follow me, and I will make you fishers of men." The implications of this verse are clear. If we follow Jesus, He will make us to be fishers of men. If we are fishers of men, it naturally means that we are followers of Christ. Therefore, we must deduce, that if we are not fishers of men, there is something wrong with our following of Him!

7

Look at His last command. In Acts 1:8 Jesus was about to return to heaven and His disciples were gathering around, not knowing what to expect. They were concerned about the restoration of the Kingdom of Israel, but He had other things in mind. He said, in His last words, "But ye shall receive power after that the Holy Ghost is come upon you: and ye shall be witnesses unto me both in Jerusalem, and in all Judea, and in Samaria, and unto the uttermost part of the earth." Evangelism Explosion, out of Dr. D. J. Kennedy's church in Ft Lauderdale, Florida, USA, has coined the phrase, "His last command our first concern" as its motto.

Then we look at His plan for the Church. When the Lord Jesus was facing the shadow of the cross, He gathered His disciples together at Caesarea Philippi. It was there that He enquired as to the opinion people had of Him, and what the disciples thought of Him. When Simon Peter, in a flash of spiritual illumination said, "Thou art the Christ, the Son of the Living God", Jesus replied and said, "Blessed art thou Simon Barjona. For flesh and blood hath not revealed it unto thee, but my Father which is in heaven. And I say also unto thee, that thou art Peter, and upon this rock I will build my church; and the gates of hell shall not prevail against it." Verse 19, "And I will give unto thee the keys of the Kingdom of Heaven: and whatsoever thou shalt bind on earth shall be bound in heaven, and whatsoever thou shalt loose on earth shall be loosed in heaven."

Jesus was obviously speaking to Peter about the faith that had just declared Him the Son of God. And it was upon that type of faith that the church would be built, and the keys of the Kingdom would be given to the church. Now keys of the Kingdom speak of that which opens the doors to the Kingdom. Surely this would be the mind and plan of the Lord Jesus that the church's task would be to use the keys in opening the doors for multitudes to enter.

It is obvious that the Main Thing is emphasized in the sayings of the Lord as we look at the *Great Commission*. This is of course found in Matt 28:18-20. While for some it has become the great omission, for others it stands as the Great Commission. Dividing the commission up, we notice the emphasis on the word "all":

- All power—the authority that is behind us.
- All nations—the arena in which we must work.
- All things—the accent of our activities.
- And the always—the accompaniment that is with us.

The operative words in the Great Commission are of course to "go" and "teach." You cannot teach until you go. The emphasis today is, "Come to church and be saved." Here it is, "Go and get them." What tremendous truths issue from those statements!

### It is Endorsed by the Angel.

In announcing the birth of the Lord Jesus, the angel said in Matt 1:21, "And she shall bring forth a Son, and thou shalt call His name JESUS: for He shall save His people from their sins."

**It is Expounded by its Terms.**

There are a number of words and terms used in the New Testament that spell out the urgency and importance of spreading the Gospel.

For instance, in Luke 2:49 Jesus said, "I must be about my Father's business." The Father's business is surely evangelism. John 3:16 says, "For God so loved the world that He gave His only begotten Son. . . . "

The main purpose in the writing of the Bible as we see it according to 1 John 5:13 is ". . . these things have I written . . . that ye may know that ye have eternal life."

## 2.2  Its Priority in the Life of Jesus

One cannot but recognize again and again, as one traces the life of the Lord Jesus, the priority of evangelism and spreading the Good News. Let's look at a few examples:

In John 4 we have the classic example of the Lord Jesus in action as He shares the Gospel with the woman at the well of Samaria. It's interesting to notice that while Jesus was sharing the Gospel, the disciples were absent. Why weren't they busy sharing? A few suggestions: Perhaps they were too busy. The Bible says they had gone to get food. Was it necessary for all of them to be carrying the food? Sometimes one can be so busy with many other things, that we miss out on doing the Main Thing. Perhaps they were too blind. In fact, Jesus had to say to them "lift up your eyes and look on the fields." They were blind to her need, blind to the opportunity. Perhaps they were too bothered that Jesus was witnessing to a Samaritan woman. He was crossing the racial barrier, gender barrier and social barriers. Maybe this bothered them slightly. Then again, perhaps they were just too afraid to speak up.

The story of the Lord Jesus and Zaccheus is worth recalling. In Luke 19 we have Jesus coming out of Jericho, and a man called Zaccheus, hiding up in a tree, wanting to see Jesus. In his inquisitiveness he did not want to be identified with Christ. But Jesus made a special point of stopping directly where he was, looking up into the tree, and calling him by his name, saying that he, Jesus, wanted to meet him. Jesus was not too busy, nor too afraid to confront and to challenge. Then what follows is the tremendous declaration of Zaccheus, "I will restore fourfold . . ." In verse 10 Jesus replied, "For the Son of Man is come to seek and to save that which was lost."

Jesus is seen in action again, as far as personal evangelism is concerned, on the cross! In Luke 23:42 the condemned criminal cried out, "Lord, remember me when Thou comest into Thy Kingdom." Then Jesus said to him, "Verily verily I say unto you, today shalt thou be with me in paradise." Here we see compassion and concern, even in the critical hours of death.

The priorities of the Lord Jesus are seen in some of His statements. Look for instance at Matt. 9:37-38, "Then saith He unto His disciples, The harvest truly is plenteous, but the labourers are few; Pray ye therefore the Lord of the harvest, that He will send forth labourers into His harvest." In this particular passage the Lord Jesus states the need and challenges the disciples. He also asks for prayer, because of the need for labourers to be sent into the harvest. Surely this is the heart of Jesus in action concerning a world that did not know Him. In fact, in verse 36 we read, "And when He saw the multitudes He was moved with compassion on them, because they fainted, and were scattered abroad, as sheep having no shepherd."

Then in John 4:35 the Lord Jesus rebukes the disciples, as we saw earlier, and says these words, "Say not ye, there are yet four months, and then cometh harvest? Behold, I say unto you, lift up your eyes, and look on the fields, for they are white already to harvest." Normally when it was harvest time the fields were golden. When it was white, it meant that they were over ripe.

This underlines something of the urgency of harvesting. Perhaps this is put in clearer terms in the prayer of the Lord Jesus as found in John 17, when He says, in verse 3, "And this is life eternal, that they might know Thee the only true God, and Jesus Christ, whom Thou hast sent."

Isn't this the Gospel in a nutshell?

## 2.3 Its Predominance in the life of Paul

Evangelism and outreach played a very real part in the apostle Paul's life. Look at it as we see it in his *making*: Acts 9:10, "This man is a chosen vessel to carry my name before the Gentiles and their kings and before the people of Israel."

His *motivation*: 2 Corinthians 5:11, "Knowing the fear of the Lord, we persuade men." In 2 Corinthians 5:14, "Christ's love compels, or constrains us . . . " In 1 Corinthians 9:22, "By all means I might save some"

Look at his *message*: 2 Corinthians 5:19, "What has been committed to us is the message of reconciliation".

Look at his *method*: in Athens, he challenged the people of the day regarding the unknown god (Acts 17:16). Then before Agrippa he asked loudly and clearly, after giving his defense, "King Agrippa, believest thou the prophets?"

## 2.4 Its Practice in the early Church

Someone said of the book of Acts that it can be described in three words—UP/DOWN/OUT: Jesus went *up*, the Holy Spirit came *down*, and the Church *went out*.

Look at a brief overview of some of the early chapters of Acts:

- In chapter one the early church received the orders for the spreading of the Gospel.
- In chapter two they proclaimed the Gospel.
- In chapter three they preached the Gospel, both before the people and to the lame man at the gate.
- In chapter four they presented the Gospel to the rulers and elders and scribes as they stood on trial.
- In chapter five they practiced the Gospel before the Sadducees.
- In chapter six they planned the spread of the Gospel in the re-organizing of the church.
- In chapter seven they paid for the Gospel, i.e. Stephen was persecuted.
- In chapter eight they partnered the Gospel, i.e. Philip went to Samaria and saw the

Gospel spread in revival blessing. This resulted in the eunuch's salvation.

- In chapter nine they provided the Gospel, i.e. for Saul. Little did they know what would happen as a result of this provision of the Gospel.

So we can go on and speak again and again of how the Gospel spread through the early church.

## 2.5 Its Power in Society

This is explained under the next main heading namely "Describing its Implications"

# 3. DESCRIBING ITS IMPLICATIONS

A writer returned 130 years ago after a trip around the world. The missionaries had been criticized, so he wrote a letter of the "Chained Savages of the South Seas": "For a voyager to forget these things is base ineptitude. Should he chance to be at the point of shipwreck on some unknown coast, he will most devotedly pray that the lesson of the missionary may have preceded him." The writer was none other than Charles Darwin. The difference is, being invited to dinner, or being the dinner.

In the next chapter we will deal with the "WHY" and will obviously amplify the implications. The implications of the MAIN THING have far reaching results! Compare two men: Max Dukes and Jonathan Edwards.

Max Dukes was an atheist, and lived a godless life. He married an ungodly girl, and from the progeny of this union there were 310 who died as paupers, 150 were criminals, seven were murderers, 100 were drunkards and more than half of the women were prostitutes.

His 540 descendants cost the State one and a quarter million US Dollars.

Jonathan Edwards was born at the same time as Max Dukes. He married a godly girl. An investigation was made of their 1394 known descendants, of which 13 became college presidents, 65 college professors, two USA senators, 30 judges, 100 lawyers, 60 physicians, 75 army and navy officers, 100 preachers and missionaries, 60 authors of prominence, one vice- president of the USA and 80 public officials in other capacities. There were 295 college graduates, among whom were governors of States, and ministers to foreign countries.

His descendants did not cost the State one cent.

In conclusion, I trust you have seen that what the Main Thing is, is very important, and that it justifies itself as being the Main Thing. It must surely issue a challenge for its restoration back into the life of the church today.

# Chapter Two

# THE MAIN THING

## WHY? - ITS PURPOSE

1. **BECAUSE OF WHAT THE MAIN THING IS ALL ABOUT**

2. **BECAUSE OF THE NEED OF THE WORLD**

    2.1 It is a **HUGE** World

    2.2 It is a **HURTING** World

    2.3 It is a **HUNGRY** World

    2.4 It is a **HOLLOW** World

    2.5 It is a **HOPELESS** World

3. **BECAUSE OF THE FAILURE OF THE CHURCH**

    3.1 The church has ignored its mandate

    3.2 The church is ignorant of the needs of the people

    3.3 The church has been impressed with modern day trends

    3.4 The church has been involved with lesser things

    3.5 The church has incorporated its own theories

4. **BECAUSE OUR LEADERSHIP IS UNDE-FINED**

5. **BECAUSE OF THE DEVIL'S COMMITMENT**

6. **BECAUSE OF THE PRICE INVOLVED**

7. **BECAUSE THE CHURCH HAS THE POTENTIAL**

8. **BECAUSE THE SPIRIT IS COMMITTED**

Let me give eight answers to this question:

## 1. BECAUSE OF WHAT THE MAIN THING IS ALL ABOUT

Although this has already been discussed in the first chapter, its very meaning justifies its acceptance. So let me press the point a little more.

In Romans 1:14-16, we have some tremendous thoughts laid out by the apostle Paul.

Verse 14, "I am debtor both to the Greeks, and to the Barbarians; both to the wise, and to the unwise."

Verse 15, "So, as much as in me is, I am ready to preach the Gospel to you that are at Rome also."

Verse 16, "For I am not ashamed of the Gospel of Christ: for it is the power of God unto salvation to everyone that believeth; to the Jew first, and also to the Greek."

These verses of course reveal what the Main Thing is.

- Verse 14—*A debt that must be paid.* Paul was in debt to Greeks, and the Barbarians, the wise and the unwise. In other words, I am indebted to everyone until I've shared the Gospel with them.

- Verse 15- *A passion that must be fulfilled.* Paul had a passion and a longing to go to preach the Gospel there also.

- Verse 16—*A message that needs no apology.* This message of the Gospel will stand alone and defy the tests that come its way.

- Verse 16—*A power that is inexhaustible.* He uses the word power, translated from the

21

Greek word *dunamis,* from which our word *dynamite* comes. Such is the extent of the power of the Gospel.

The Main Thing is the Main Thing, simply because of what this Main Thing is. It is t*he power of God unto salvation.*

Can you imagine a Christian who is supposed to be loving and caring, visiting a lady who is dreadfully ill with cancer. The Christian visits the lady and has in her bag a bottle that contains a certain medicine that could cure cancer once and for all. Can you imagine her visiting, talking, reading, doing everything else, but never giving the lady the cure that could save her life.

For someone who was not loving, we could understand that , but for someone who is loving and called a Christian, and has such a bottle of cure, and does not share it, we would regard such a person as a monster! Maybe that is what some do with the message of salvation today.

## 2. BECAUSE OF THE NEED OF THE WORLD

Let me share with you something about this world in which we live.

### 2.1 It is a HUGE World.

I was impressed the other day to hear that the world population at the present moment is just over six billion people. At the present rate of 240,000 more births than deaths a day, this will double our population every 40 years, thus reaching 24 billion in the life time of those living today! Startling isn't it?

## 2.2 It is a HURTING World.

One hardly needs to elaborate on the fact that in spite of all of our development in the areas of science and technology, and with modern comforts etc., there is still so much hurt around. Little children, men, women, couples, and nations are hurting today. It's a *hurting world.*

## 2.3 It is a HUNGRY World.

It seems to be such a tragedy that while almost half of the world lives with too much to eat and throws so much away, others are starving to death. There's just so much malnutrition. This is not only a physically hungry world, but let me suggest that it is also spiritually hungry. The world is confused. While the East asks "which god?", the West is saying, "why God?"

## 2.4 It is a HOLLOW World.

The world seems to be smiling on the outside, but crying on the inside. Our cleverness, developments, sophistication, and wealth have not been able to come up with that Utopia for which man seeks; therefore, people are still hollow today.

And of course

## 2.5 It is a HOPELESS World.

The world cries for hope. "Is there any hope?" is the longing that comes from the hearts of politicians and peasants alike. We certainly live in a world which needs healing for the past, help for the present, and hope for the future.

Well may we agree with the little chorus:

Tell all the world there is sight for its blindness,
Balm for its healing, and a song for its dumb,
Blood for its cleansing, and life for its dying;
Tell them of Jesus, and bid them to come.

Surely the desperate need of our world is enough for the church, and for us all, to realize that the Main Thing is to accelerate the spread of the Gospel as quickly as possible.

## 3. BECAUSE OF THE FAILURE OF THE CHURCH

This may be the greatest reason, or the most tragic reason of all. Someone once said, and I quote, "What breaks the heart of God more, is a world that will not come, or a church that will not go!"

### 3.1 The Church has ignored its mandate.

Someone has well said, "The health curve of the church throughout the centuries, can pretty well be plotted by the warmth of its evangelistic fervor." Another warns, "When Christians fail to evangelize, the very existence of the church is threatened."

Evangelism Explosion is one of God's tools today, in seeking to win the world to Christ. It is the one organization that has its ministry in every single nation of the world. One of its basic tenets is to stress the importance of the biblical principles of evangelism.

24

Let me share them with you:

**The church is an army under orders. As an army it must be going forward and fighting the battle.**

In Matt. 4:19 we have the great call. This has already been mentioned in a previous chapter. "Follow me and I will make you fishers of men." In Matt. 28:18-20 we have the Great Commission. The operative word is "go". We have the Great Command in Acts 1:8. The sign of the Holy Spirit's abiding within our hearts is that we will be witnesses unto Christ.

**The pastor is the general in charge.**

Eph 4:11-12: "And He gave gifts unto the church."

One of the gifts of leadership, is that of the pastor. This is for the "equipping of the saints to do the work of the ministry." The general does not do all the work, but he plans, strategizes, and sees that his men are equipped to do the task.

**The laymen are the combat troops.**

In Acts 8:1 we read, "And at that time there was a great persecution against the church which was scattered at Jerusalem; and they were all scattered abroad throughout the regions of Judea and Samaria, except the apostles". Verse 4 says, "Therefore they that were scattered abroad went everywhere preaching the word." A better translation would be "went everywhere gossiping the word." The apostles stayed at home-base while the laymen—the church workers etc., were scattered abroad. This scattering was not only because of the persecution, but was God's way in using the sever-

ity of persecution to see the Gospel spreading throughout the then known world.

### The Gospel is the weapon.

Romans 1:16. "I am not ashamed of the Gospel of
Christ"

Every soldier has a weapon. He must know how to
use it.

### Victory depends on on-the-job training.

It is not enough for the soldier to know the work in
theory. He needs to know how to do it on the battle-
field. In Mark 3:14 we read, "And He ordained twelve,
that they should be with Him, and that He might send
them forth to preach. . . ." The operative expression
there is, "that they may be with Him". Before He ever
dared to send them out, they had to learn from Him, in
what is called "on-the-job" training.

### The best form of evangelism is multiplication.

We can try to win people by additions, but multiplication makes it so much faster. Acts 6:7, "And the word
of God increased; and the number of the disciples multi-
plied in Jerusalem greatly; and a great company of the
priests were obedient to the faith." The multiplication of
the disciples was the decisive factor. If you take the life
of Jesus, He ministered to one disciple that He loved
dearly—that was John. Then there were three who were
regarded as very close to Him, Peter, James and John.
The circle gets bigger with the twelve disciples. Then,
He sent out seventy to go amongst the villagers and
share the Gospel. Then, as we know, it became 120 on

the day of Pentecost, when they were gathered in the upper room. On the day of Pentecost, 3,000 were added to the church, so the circles grew bigger. Then we read of 5,000. Later, commentators say over 10, 000 had come to Christ in those first few years of the early church's functioning. That's the circle effect of multiplication!

## 3.2 The church is ignorant of the needs of the people.

In his tremendous book *Hitler's Cross*,[1] Erwin Lutzer tells the story of a small church near a railroad track. He writes that each Sunday they would hear the whistle in the distance and the wheels coming over the tracks. As a church they were disturbed when they heard the cries coming from the train as it passed by. They realized that it was carrying Jews like cattle in the cars. Week after week the whistle would blow. They dreaded to hear the sound of those wheels because they knew they would hear the cries of the Jews en route to a death camp. Their screams tormented them.

When they eventually heard the trains coming, they would begin to sing hymns. By the time the train came past the church, they were singing at the tops of their voices. If they heard any screams they would sing even louder. Soon they would hear them no more. He says that many of them, by the singing of the hymns, never heard the cries of those on their way to be slaughtered. Is that perhaps what the church has done over the years?

It is possible that we have become ignorant because of our involvement in our own affairs, and that the needs and cries of the world outside have fallen on deaf ears.

### 3.3 **The church has been impressed with modern day trends.**

I think it is absolutely essential that the church bear in mind that old slogan "Anchored to the Rock, geared to the times." The church must keep abreast with what is developing, but we cannot allow the influence of the world to infiltrate it.

Let's face it, church growth "has become a popular topic." Anyone who has a formula for growing a church quickly becomes a sought-after speaker. More people are attending conferences and buying books than ever before. However, there are fewer results. The fact of the matter is that in spite of much knowledge about church growth, etc., it doesn't seem to be working.

What are the reasons?

- Do we blame the consultants and their methods? Have they misled us? Are they talking about "airy fairy" ideas and dreams? That might be a factor.

- Is it the denominational structures? We have seen a new wave of independent churches developing under their own leadership, devoid of any accountability. Have the denomina tional structures stunted church growth?

- Well, maybe the problems lie with our seminaries? Someone may say that there is too much academic teaching.

- Another says, "Well really it's the local pastor—he's lazy, depends on gimmicks, is an excellent delegator, and has a lack of passion."

- Another comes along and says, "Well, that may be a reason, but I think the reason is that the local people are tired, lazy, and apathetic."

- Another says, "It's the materialistic world in which we live. Therefore we can't go ahead."

I think the answer lies in what one writer has said, "Our problem is a spiritual problem not one of methodology."

If we take the Great Commission and align ourselves, our emphasis, and our activities against it, where do we stand? Let me give some examples which will perhaps indicate just how far we have moved away from the responsibilities attached to the Great Commission, as far as our churches are concerned.

Suppose that at a deacons' or church council meeting a worker came in and said, "Last night ten people came to Christ as a result of our visitation program!" What would the general response be? I can hear someone saying, "That's good, but will they stand?" Another says, "Well we've heard that before, but where are the results?" Others will say, "Good work brother, keep it up" (Don't involve us).

Take the same group and tell them that last night the church received a hundred thousand Dollars or Pounds, and what response would you get? I think the treasurer would probably shout hallelujah and do a back flip. What does that tell us? There is far more enthusiasm when money comes into the church, than when people come to Christ!

Take another situation. Instead of ten people coming to Christ last night, the report is that ten were healed, or ten spoke in tongues! What would be the response? In many churches there would be far more enthusiasm to hear of ten being healed, or speaking in tongues, than of ten being saved. What am I trying to say? I'm trying to say that we can easily be diverted by other things, other than "the Main Thing".

### 3.4 The church has been involved with lesser things.

We need to be careful that we do not get bogged down with the multiplicity of duties that even atheists can do, but neglecting the things that only the supernatural power of Jesus Christ can do by His Spirit, through His bride, the local church.

Maybe the involvement with lesser things is because we have taken our eyes off the Main Thing.

Someone has well said, "The unwilling are voted in by the unfit, to do the unnecessary." Is that true of your church or mine? Maybe we have failed in our very integrity, and therefore brought a lack of authenticity to our evangelism. The Bible speaks of us being the salt of the earth and the light of the world. Bill Hybles, who has seen a remarkable explosion in his church, seems to put his finger on a very key point, and that is "authenticity in the local church for evangelism." He says, "Christians are to *be* good news before they *share* the Good News.

You see, this is the age where we rationalize our short-comings, cover our tracks, and hire successful attorneys to get us off the hook. It was Mahatma Ghandi who said, "I might have been a Christian if it weren't for the Christians!"

Our involvement in lesser things, instead of the Main Thing, has perhaps weakened our integrity in the community.

## 3.5 The church has incorporated its theories.

Pet theories, personal views, prejudiced views, and even theological view points, have perhaps hindered the proclamation and furtherance of the Gospel.

For instance :

- There are those who say that not all are called to evangelism, so we must not put pressure on people to do evangelism. I think that is true; not all have the gift of evangelism but all are called to be witnesses, according to Acts 1:8. Therefore it is the job of the church to train and equip our people to be witnesses.

- Some see evangelism as a department. In many churches, and even denominations, evangelism is a separate department for those who might be interested. It becomes comparable to the men's department, the missions department, the women's department, and the music department. Evangelism is not a department; it is a ministry. It is the church spreading into each of the departments, bringing life, meaning, purpose, and direction to the women's department, to the men's department, the music department, etc.

- Many of us have replaced the Main Thing with other concerns which may be good, such as social concerns. Perhaps evangelicals can be accused of not being concerned enough on the social level. However, we need to make sure that our social concern is the outcome of our evangelistic concern. Many started off as good, thorough evangelicals, but have become consumed with social concerns, and forgotten that caring for the body is one thing, but caring for the soul lasts for all eternity!

## 4. BECAUSE OUR LEADERSHIP IS UNDEFINED

We will be studying this in greater depth when we look at the "WHO" of the Main Thing.

Most pastors are expected to be leaders, but unfortunately they are not leading. If some are leading, they are leading as dictators, and that is also unacceptable. Leadership by example is the crying need today. So many of our people know that they must witness, know that they must pray, know that they must serve God, but their cry is—"pastor, please show us how."

Is it possible that we are busy with 101 things the Lord never asked us to do, except the one thing He asked us to do, to make disciples?

Eph. 4 deals with the question of gifts of leadership given by the Lord Jesus to the early church.

Verses 11-12, "And He gave some, apostles; and some, prophets; and some, evangelists; and some, pastors and teachers; for the perfecting of the saints, for the work of the ministry." It is right here where this verse is dubbed the "verse of the error of the comma." In the original there is no comma after "the saints", so it should rather read "for the perfecting of the saints for the work of the ministry. . . ."

Here the pastor is seen as an equipper of the saints. The coach concept is helpful here. In our church, when I was busy training our people to be evangelists and witnesses for Christ, they eventually caught the idea of Eph. 4, and called me "Coach Peasley."

In his book *Up With Worship*, Ray Ortland says that the church today has certainly gone wrong, and it is likened to a modern-day theatre. We have those who pay and want to be entertained. On the platform is someone seeking to entertain them, and behind are the prompters.

The analogy is, that our members and people in the pew pay to attend, sit where they want to, clap at what they enjoy, and stamp their feet at what they do not like.

On the platform is a little man who does his best to keep them entertained. He is always thinking of some new trick, plan, or idea to keep them happy. But behind him are the prompters who keep on telling him what he must do. If he speaks too loudly, they say he needs to speak more softly, if he speaks for too short a time, they say he needs to speak longer, etc. Eventually the little man on the platform is tired out, torn between the prompters and the spectators.

Ortland says unfortunately that is a picture of the modern-day church. The pastor or preacher is simply trying to keep his people happy, and he is constantly prompted by the council, or elders, or deacons' board.

In the true picture of the church, the pastor is the prompter, and if that is true, then who is on the platform? It is our members, the disciples, those whom we are equipping, prompting to perform for whoever is in the audience. And who is in the audience? None other than God!

Therefore, it is your job as a pastor, or my job as a preacher, to prompt our people, train them, and equip them, so that they may please God.

## 5. BECAUSE OF THE DEVIL'S COMMITMENT

The devil has been around for a long, long time.

Look at his past experience. The Bible tells us that he was thrown out of heaven. He therefore has a good idea about heaven, God and the celestial sphere. He was cast into hell, and he is well aware of the effects and the torments of hell.

Because he knows about God and the celestial sphere, hell and its final damnation, and because he knows of the meaning of the cross, and that he is ultimately defeated, that his time is limited, the Bible tells us that "he goes about as a roaring lion."

He also knows that the keys of the Kingdom are given to the church—that is, to open the doors for people to get in, and so his one objective is to keep as many people as possible out of the Kingdom. He has won many friends and many followers, and he encourages them to encourage others not to be involved in evangelism, or the Main Thing. He knows that if he can keep them away f rom the Main Thing, he can divert others to hell, instead of to heaven.

Unfortunately, too many today have fallen to his subtle suggestions, his substitutes for evangelism, and his sinister offers of earthly rewards.

## 6. BECAUSE OF THE PRICE INVOLVED IN FULFILLING THE GREAT COMMISSION.

While salvation is free, living it out costs us everything. Let me mention three :

- *Commitment.* In Evangelism Explosion, the word "FAT" is taught to those who are seeking to be trained in evangelism. It simply means "Faithful—Available—Teachable."

- *Faith.* Our life is dependent upon God. We are called to live a life of faith. We are called to be faithful.

- *Obedient.* The commission is not there as an option. The great command in Acts 8 is not just for the disciples, but for us today.

On the north coast of America, there was a coastal village where many ships were wrecked. So many had sunk that they built a coast-guard station there.

One night the alarm sounded and the lights went on, and they knew that a ship was wrecked. The coast-guard called all helpers to go out and assist with the rescue. When the life-boats were ready, one of the sailors came back and said it was impossible; the waves were 15 feet high and they would never make it. The coast-guard replied, "I told you to man the boats." A little later the lieutenant came and saw that it was impossible, and like the sailor, said to the coast-guard,

"It is so bad out there, even if we get out, we will never make it back." The coast-guard said, "Bowser, the command is, we have to go. We don't have to come back!"

If that was the attitude of a coast-guard to help rescue the perishing, how much more should it be ours, who claim to be followers of the Lord Jesus. That is commitment.

## 7. BECAUSE THE CHURCH HAS THE POTENTIAL

The *message* that is committed to the church is not static but dynamic. It is a message we need never be ashamed of, and as Paul says, "It is the power of God unto salvation." "Faith cometh by hearing, and hearing by the word of God." Romans 10:17.

Look at its *manpower*. The church has gifted men and women from all walks of society. These gifts have been given by the Spirit, so that believers may be equipped to reach and touch others effectively in their community.

Thirdly, look at its *methodology*. The early church never slacked in its outreach, and used any methods of spreading the Gospel, gossiping the Gospel, that would simply tell others about the Gospel. Paul longed that "by all means I may win some."

Then look at its *Master*. The One going ahead, is none other than Jesus. He set the pace, gave the command, and we are to follow.

## 8. BECAUSE THE SPIRIT IS COMMITTED

The Holy Spirit, being Who He is, is committed to the spreading of the Gospel around the world today. In

fact, we have been amazed at some of the most remarkable developments in recent times. In his book, *The
Gates of Hell Shall not Prevail²*, Dr. James Kennedy says,
"When Jesus Christ died and rose from the dead, there
were some 120 believers who had gathered in an upper
room to pray. . . .

"When Peter preached a sermon, there were 3,000
who believed. Shortly thereafter 5,000 more were
added to the church . . .

"Next came the time of persecution, and when it
ended in AD 313 with the edict of toleration, there were
about 10 million professing Christians alive." By the
year 1000, this number had grown to 50 million. By the
end of the 18th century, most of the missionary endeav-
ors had stalled, yet the number had grown to 215 million professing Christians. That is an increase of 165
million in 800 years.

In 1795 the modern missionary movement began
in earnest with William Carey. By the year 1900, there
were 500 million professing Christians. That is an
increase of 285 million in one century. Then by 1980,
just 80 short years later, that number had grown to 1.3
billion professing Christians. Then by 1900, that number had grown to roughly 1.8 billion—an increase of 1.3
billion people in the 20th century alone. (These figures
are given by the US Centre for World Missions in
Pasadena, California).

Dr. David Barrett, probably the greatest church
statistician alive, states, "Today 540 million out of 54 billion people in the world are Bible-believing Christians."

All this and more, tells us that the Holy Spirit is
committed to honor every single person, church,

organization, mission, and ministry, that seeks to fulfill the Great Commission.

Surely the challenge is up to us, to grasp it with both hands.

We need no further reasoning as to the "WHY" of the Main Thing!

# Chapter Three

# THE MAIN THING

## WHO? - ITS PEOPLE

1. **A LOVING GOD**

2. **NEEDY SINNERS**

3. **WILLING WORKERS :**

    **3:1  The Leadership Factor**

    **3:2  The Laity Factor**

    **3:3  The Multiplication Factor**

    **3:4  The Charisma Factor**

    **3:5  The Spirit Factor**

The question of "Who" is involved, is vital because without it the "WHAT" and 'WHY" would be superfluous.

Whenever evangelism takes place, there are three Principles/People that come into operation:

- A loving God
- Needy sinners
- Willing workers

Acts 8 tells of the amazing conversion of the eunuch in the desert. There was certainly a *loving God* in operation who brought together Philip and the eunuch. The *needy sinner* is of course the eunuch, and the *willing worker* is Philip. Remember, Philip came out of revival in Samaria to wander around in the desert, waiting for God to show him what was next on the divine agenda.

Acts 9 tells us of the amazing conversion of Saul of Tarsus. Once again we have a *loving God* in operation. In spite of Saul's attitude against the church, he never dreamed what was going to happen to him on that road to Damascus. A shining light struck him down, blinded him, and he was led into the city. Here was God extending love and mercy toward a persecutor of the church! Saul was of course the *needy sinner.*

The *willing worker* is seen in the person of Ananias, who was found in the place of prayer when God used him. He was obedient and willing to go, even though it was to the persecutor of the church. He showed courage, faith and obedience: the true marks of a *willing worker.*

In Acts 10 we have the story of Cornelius, the captain of the Italian band at Caesarea. He was a *needy man*

43

and God put him and Peter together. Peter, while praying, was found to be a *willing worker.* He went and proclaimed the Gospel to the Gentiles. Who knows what would have happened if Peter had not been *willing?*

Let's enlarge on these thoughts.

## 1.   A LOVING GOD

It is the nature of God to love. The greatest verse in the Bible is surely John 3:16 "For God so loved the world . . ." It was His love that caused Him to send His only Son to die on the cross. Everything about God is love. It emanates from Him. All He does, is because He loves. Two illustrations suffice.

In the Garden of Eden, when Adam and Eve had failed and then hid themselves because of guilt, God, in His love and mercy, went after them, and walked in the garden and called after them. He even made them clothes to wear to cover their shame. Surely that is a *loving God* in action.

On the Cross of Calvary, we have a personification of the love of God. Here was God going all the way to reach out and redeem us to Himself. He sent His only beloved Son to do this. There is no doubt in our minds, that God in His sovereignty and divine power is loving and compassionate, and is concerned for all. Surely in the heart and mind of God, is the evangelization of the world.

## 2.   NEEDY SINNERS

They are everywhere. In fact, "all have sinned and come short of the glory of God."

You will find them hiding in the sycamore trees, at the wells of Sychar in Samaria, dying on a cross, on a road to Damascus, travelling in the desert, etc. There are needs that are abounding. It is interesting to read in Luke 19:41 that the Lord Jesus wept over the city of Jerusalem. He saw Jerusalem as more than an historic city, more than just an international city—it was a city of *needy people*.

As the saying goes :

Cities are more than steel and stone,
Or humming wheels and towers adrone;
Cities are more than block-long stores
With neon-signs and countless doors.
Cities have eyes afire with tears
And hearts that flee the mocking years;
Ears that hear no sound of song,
Feet that stumble on streets of wrong.
Cities are full of children crying,
Cities are full of people dying,
Cities are souls for whom He died.

It is said of the 5.2 billion people inhabiting the world today:

- 1.8 billion are undernourished
- 500 million are severely malnourished
- 20 million die from starvation-related deaths per annum
- 4 million are political prisoners
- 1 million are prisoners for religious reasons
- 100 000 prisoners are tortured per annum
- 300 000 martyrs die per annum

- 32 million are slaves
- 850 000 murders occur every year
- 2.6 billion are denied religious freedom
- 3 billion are denied freedom to travel in other countries
- 4 billion are denied full political freedom

The costs of sin are revealed by the figures released by the Source for World Evangelism data-base :

- Pornography costs America 20 billion dollars a year
- The drug traffic costs 150 billion dollars a year
- Gambling costs 700 billion dollars a year
- Fraud costs 800 billion dollars
- Theft costs 3200 billion dollars

Surely "the wages of sin is death."

William Booth, the founder of the Salvation Army, who spent his life caring for those who were in need, said :

"While women weep as they do now—I'll fight
While little children go hungry—I'll fight
While men go to prison, in and out—I'll fight
While there is a drunkard left—I'll fight
While there is a poor lost girl on the streets—I'll fight
While there remains one dark soul without the light of God—I'll fight, I'll fight,
I'll fight to the very end."

We live in a world where there is a birth every 2.8 seconds, where 10, 350 people are born every hour, 247, 000 every day, 90 million every year.

Almost 60% of all people who ever lived, are alive to-day. Of close to six-billion people in the world, almost four-billion have never heard the name of Jesus Christ. 150, 000 are dying daily without Christ. (Taken from Intercessory Prayer Ministry, Bellevue Baptist Church, Cordova Tennessee, USA).

I don't think we need to belabor the point any longer on the desperate needs surrounding us to-day.

## 3. WILLING WORKERS

The biggest area of concern is not the fact of our loving God, or the needy sinners, but rather the *willing workers*. As Bonar said, "No soul will be in heaven without a human thumb mark upon it!"

If we are to look at willing workers, where should we start? Surely with the leader.

### 3:1 The Leadership Factor :

Down through the years, this old world has seen many leaders. Perhaps one of the most renowned was Adolf Hitler. Here was a man who used the word "democracy" to establish dictatorship.

We are told that he so captivated the minds of the German people, that even Winston Churchill observed, in 1937, that Hitler's accomplishments "were amongst the most remarkable in the whole history of the world."

In his day, Christians took the picture of Christ from the walls in their homes and replaced it with a portrait of Hitler! His leadership extended to the place

47

where he had the German people surrendering their personal rights, and implementing laws that led to the extermination of more than eight million people. It resulted in a war where over 50 million people were killed in the greatest blood-bath in history. Before he died, we are told, thousands of pastors had joined the SS troops in swearing personal allegiance to him! That's leadership for you! But our Leader—the greatest leader of all the Lord Jesus Christ, exercised another form of leadership. In the area of evangelism, He led the way. He was not too busy to meet the needs of little children and said "Suffer the little children to come unto Me." He took time at the cross to express concern for the care of His mother. He stopped, even while carrying the cross, and gave words of comfort to the women who were weeping. In the area of evangelism, it was Jesus who set the pace when He said "For the Son of man is come to seek and to save that which was lost."

Paul was, of course, another great example. While in Athens, and waiting for company to join him, he entered into a discussion regarding "the unknown god." While in Caesar's palace, he was able to witness even to the Praetorium guard! He challenged king Agrippa as to his belief in Jesus Christ. In Philippi he was used to win a demonic slave—from the lowest strata of society—to deliverance in Jesus Christ. A hardened, cold, callous, cruel jailer came to Christ when this man refused to escape. And the well-to-do, but good business lady Lydia, had her heart opened to the Gospel when confronted with the challenges of Paul the apostle.

Peter was an evangelist. On the day of Pentecost, this man, who had run away before a little girl, now stood up and spoke boldly about Christ, and even told the Jewish people "Him. . . . ye have taken, and by wicked hands have crucified and slain: Whom God hath raised up". He was an evangelist. Maybe it started when Jesus met him and asked him at the sea of Galilee, "lovest thou Me?" Peter's reply was "yes I like You." You see there is a play on words there between *agape* love and *phileo* love. Phileo love is 'yes I like you for what I can get out of you'.

In John 21:15 we read "So when they had dined, Jesus saith to Simon Peter, Simon, son of Jonas, lovest thou Me more than these? (Do you *agape* Me?)

He saith unto Him "Yea Lord; Thou knowest that I love Thee." (*Phileo* you.)

He saith unto him, Feed my lambs".

Then Jesus asked him again, a third time, and eventually Peter realized that Jesus was wringing out of him the fact that *phileo* was not enough, but that he needed to come clean and have a love which was totally committed to Him. Jesus then said, not only "feed my lambs" but twice "feed my sheep". Maybe that's where it all starts as a leader. We are to be filled with love—*agape* love committed to Christ no matter what the cost.

In Eph. 4 we have that remarkable passage, which we have already commented on, regarding the whole gift of leadership. It is there where the purpose is given for the gifts of apostles, prophets, evangelists, pastors, and teachers. They are "for the perfecting (equipping) of the saints for the work of the ministry."

Surely our task as pastors and leaders is to see that our laity are equipped, so that they can be strong in sharing their faith, and knowing how to witness, apart from the other aspects of the ministry. One day, before God, we will most surely have to give an account as to how we equipped the flock.

### 3:2 The Laity Factor :

As the leader, so the laity. If the leader is a worker, the laymen will be workers. If the leader is lazy, the laity will be lazy. As the leader goes, so the layman goes. What a responsibility!

One of the finest books on the whole subject of equipping the laity for the work of the ministry is by Dr. Robert Coleman, *The Master Plan of Evangelism*.[3] He devotes an entire book to showing how the Lord Jesus spent His three-and-a-half years of public ministry in praying for His disciples, selecting His disciples, and then training and equipping them, so that when He finally departed, they would continue the vision and the plan that He had for world evangelism.

In that public ministry, 70% of His time was spent with the disciples in training, encouraging and equipping them. Surely if Jesus did this, how much more ought we to do it!

It is interesting that He loved *one* in particular, namely John. Then the circle became a little bigger, and there were *three* that He dealt with more closely—Peter, James and John. The circle increased to the *12,* and later to *70,* who were sent out to preach the Gospel. On the day of Pentecost in the upper room, the circle grew to *120.* Then came a quantum leap to *3,000,* as the circle expanded to include the many that came to faith in Christ on the day of Pentecost. Later we are told that it was *5,000,* and commentators say that over *10,000* came to Christ in the early days of the church in the book of Acts of the Apostles. The idea of the circles, starting with one to three, to 12, to 70, to 120, to 3,000, to 5,000 or 10,000, surely reveals a master plan of impacting the world and training the laity.

Most of our churches could be divided into three circles which would represent the make up of our membership today. The dots in the *outer circle* would represent those who are members, but not involved. They come, but not very frequently. I regard them as "regular"—they never miss Christmas, never miss Easter, and of course are at funerals and weddings. They demand much time of our pastors and leaders. We run after them, we nurse them, we have to put out all the fires they start, yet these are unproductive members. In spite of the enormous amount of time and energy spent with them, they are not productive and hardly responsive to the Word. Many a pastor spends his entire ministry looking after this *outer circle* of people. They frustrate him, and leave him unfulfilled.

The next circle includes those who are "nice" people. They attend twice a month. They give to the church when there is a need. They enjoy what is going on, but don't stand on their toes! They are half-involved. They attend what suits them. They enjoy looking on. They can be your best supporter one day, and your worst the next.

Thirdly, we have the *inner circle.* These unfortunately get the least attention of the pastor, but actually deserve the most. These are the "responsive", "reproductive" people; they never miss church. Their lives are the epitome of what God requires of a believer.

The question is, where should the leader or the pastor spend most of his time? Normally he spends time with the *outer circle*—the unproductive people—but he should really be spending time with the *inner circle,* as did Jesus, and his goal should be to enlarge the *inner circle* until the *outer circle* is enveloped in that plan of discipleship and evangelism. Perhaps the Great Commission is all about that "to go and to make disciples." That is when ministry is fulfilling and not frustrating.

This is what our people are waiting for. They want to be trained and shown how, but somehow our leaders have a wrong perspective of what the ministry involves. This will be elaborated in the next chapter, dealing with the HOW of the Main Thing.

### 3:3 The Multiplication Factor :

There is a large difference between multiplication and addition. If I win one person to Christ a month, over 12 months, I would have won 12. If I train one person to win two others, that means there are now three people involved—over 12 months that amounts to 36.

In South Africa, our goal is to train at least 500 key leaders every year. The responsibility is for them to train at least four others in evangelism over 12 months. A simple exercise in mathematics tells us, that if 500 are trained a year, and they each train four others in evangelism, over 2,000 are involved per year, who are trained and equipped in evangelism and personal work. If each of them had to lead one person to Christ a month, we would see the power of multiplication, with

12 times 2,000 equalling 24,000. Surely the emphasis should be put on the *multiplication factor.*

How will the world ever be reached by additions only? Let's involve ourselves in multiplication.

## 3:4 The Charisma Factor :

By this we mean the grace gifts. Our people are gifted in various ways. Just as their faces are different, so their gifts differ. Therefore, our job is to develop their gifts and to equip them for the propagation of the Gospel. A person who has the gift of hospitality should be encouraged to use that gift. Some have the gift of leadership, others have the gift of stewardship, while others have the gifts of caring, concern and compassion. What a responsibility to develop those gifts, so that God may be glorified.

## 3:5 The Spirit Factor :

Amongst our *willing workers,* nothing will really happen, or it will become merely theoretical, if we do not allow for the Spirit. All our training, equipping, theorizing and strategizing fall flat if the Spirit is not operating. The Holy Spirit enables us to do what we could not do by ourselves.

The Holy Spirit anoints us, creates opportunities, and wants to use us mightily. He equips, energizes, enables and encourages us.

In Mark 2 we have the beautiful story of the four men who brought their friend to Jesus.

The paralyzed man represents the *needy sinner;* the Lord Jesus of course represents the *loving God.* The four friends represent the *willing workers.* Notice something special about them. I would suggest that first of all they must have known Jesus. There is no way they would have brought their friend to Jesus if they had not known Him personally.

Secondly, they believed in Jesus and what He could do. It was such confidence in Jesus that caused them to bring their paralytic friend to the feet of Jesus. We notice that they wouldn't take "no" for an answer. Maybe the paralyzed man said "Now listen, I've been here for a long time. I've tried doctors; none have succeeded. Don't waste my time now." This did not deter these four men. They were determined to bring their friend to Jesus.

They didn't care what others thought. When they came to the house it was full, jam-packed and, they could not get in. They then decided to lower the man through the roof. Can you imagine what people thought. "Aren't they going too far?" "Aren't they being a bit fanatical?" They didn't care what others thought. One overwhelming obsession was theirs—to bring their friend to Jesus.

We notice that they were not bothered by the obstacles. The house was full, but part of a roof could be removed. As someone said, "they may have removed the roof, but another had to pay for it."

Some old treasurer may have said "but this is going to cost a lot of money, what are you trying to do?"

They weren't concerned with that. One thing mattered—to bring their friend to Jesus.

Then notice, they let him down exactly, precisely at Jesus' feet. That's precision in work. They were careful, concerned and committed in the way they brought their friend to Jesus.

When that friend was left at Jesus' feet, the spotlight now focused only on what happened inside the house. Never again do we hear about the men. They fade into oblivion. But they knew they had done their task. What had they done? They had brought a friend to Jesus. Surely that is what the *willing worker* is all about.

# Chapter Four

# THE MAIN THING

## HOW? - ITS PRACTICE

1. A VISION

2. A STRATEGIC PLAN

3. A PLAN OF ACTION

4. PRACTICAL SUGGESTIONS:

   4:1 Witnessing

   4:2 Church Services

   4:3 Outreaches

   4:4 Follow-up

We have looked at the "What" and the "Why" of the Main Thing, and trust that by now there is no doubt that evangelism and outreach should be the heartbeat of the church.

Now we want to move from the theory to the practice. Implementation is the name of the game.

Here are some important factors to follow :

## 1. A VISION.

The Bible says in Prov 28:18 "Where there is no vision, the people perish."

Every Christian needs to establish a vision for the work to which he or she is called.

A dream becomes a vision, a vision becomes a conviction, and the conviction results in action.

First, our vision needs to be biblically based. The theory and practice of evangelism are clearly set out in the Scriptures.

Secondly, our vision must envisage a target group. Precisely which people will we reach? The following survey was conducted by the Institute for American Church Growth, it was learned that :

- 2 % came to Christ through a special need.
- 3% came to Christ through just walking into the church.
- 6% came to Christ through a pastor.
- 1% came to Christ through visitation.
- 5% came to Christ through a Sunday School.
- 1% came to Christ through an evangelistic crusade.

- 3% came to Christ through a church program.
- 79% came to Christ through a friend/relative! Why is this response so high?
    - The Gospel is shared by a trusted friend.
    - The sharing is usually unhurried and natural.
    - A known life-style adds credibility to the witness.
    - The witness, being a friend, is a natural source for nurture.
    - The witness' church provides effective help in assimilation.

Thirdly, our vision will arise out of the challenges of the day, and the responsibilities of the church.

Someone has asked, "What is 750,000 miles (1.2 million km) long, reaches around the world 30 times, and grows 20 miles everyday?" The line of people dying every day without Christ! That is the obvious need.

The challenge of relating effectively to the range of cultural, generational and socio-economic groups in contemporary society remains critical for the churches.

Fourthly, our vision should be based on *critical factors* for church growth. In 1996, Australian churches held a National Church Life Survey covering over 312,000 attendees, and 6,700 Congregations from 23 denominations. It revealed challenges and opportunities for the Church in times of continuous change. It identified areas for growth such as the need to have :

- A growing sense of belonging.

- A commitment to the congregation's vision for the future.
- A sense of support for the leadership.
- An inspirational and directive leadership.
- Satisfaction with worship services.
- Freedom to discuss faith, and invite others to church.
- Moments of decisive faith commitment.
- Participation in nurturing activities.
- A plan for the congregation to connect faith with attendees' lives.

## 2. A STRATEGIC PLAN FOR THE CHURCH.

Once the vision has been established, a strategic plan is the next step. Several ways to achieve this strategic plan are :

- Establish potential of areas, i.e. in five, ten, 20 years' time.
- Identify types of people in the area, i.e. youth, young couples, yuppies, many children, lonely people, etc.
- Identify needs of the area.
- Establish available resources, facilities, etc., to meet needs.
- Determine quality and quantity of gifts, talents, finance etc., available.

- Establish time frame of operation, i.e. by such-and-such a time church is hoped to be thus far.
- Identify strengths and weaknesses of the church.
- Set definite goals.
- Challenge the leaders. One pastor took his leaders on a retreat. He asked them, "Suppose we had 100,000 Dollars/Pounds given to us as a church. What would we do with that amount of money?" Once they came up with various answers, he said, "Now let's imagine our situation without that money. Your answers become our goals."
- Establish spiritual values and strengths, i.e. faith, need for prayer, etc. This will bring about perspective and an outward, or outgoing plan for the church.
- Establish the true place of the working of the Holy Spirit—energizing for prayer, evangelism outreach, etc.

You may need to consider a strategic plan for your own church, and let it permeate all of your operations.

## 3. A PLAN OF ACTION.

Before we look at the practical aspects and activities, we need a definite strategy of implementation and mobilization.

An interesting study can be made in Acts 19, where Paul was in Ephesus. After witnessing boldly in the synagogue for three months (verse 8), there was opposition, so he withdrew to the school of Tyrannus (verse 9), and for two years concentrated on teaching the disciples. It was then that all Asia could be impacted with the Word (verse 10).

This leads us to develop the thought of the three circles as mentioned in the previous chapters.

## Identifying the three areas.

Most churches are divided into three main groups of membership:

- *Outer group:* these are the non-productive church members.
- *Central group:* they are attendees but not really committed.
- *Inner core:* they are called the "company of the committed."

Maybe you can categorize your membership accordingly.

## Involving the groups.

Group {a} *Outer group.* These are those that you pray for but scarcely pray with. You witness to them but not with them.

A record should be kept of your contacts with them. A record should be kept of their activities.

Availability is essential, especially in time of need. Don't expect much in return, but always go the extra mile. On special days and occasions in their lives, make sure they are contacted. If they are members of the church, make sure that a record of their attendance at church is kept, and how many times you have visited them. The goal of the church is to graduate these to group {b}.

Group {b} *The uninvolved.* They will probably attend two to three times a month. Attempts to involve them in more activities should be made from time to time. They need to be aware of what is going on in the church, and records should be kept of their attendance and involvement. As they are made to feel wanted, and their gifts are discussed, one would hope that changes would come, and they would gradually graduate to group {c}.

Group {c} Take time with them. Disciple them. Pray with them. Teach them the Word.

Identify their gifts and encourage them to use them. Don't overwork them.

Your goal as a pastor or leader is to graduate as many as possible from {a} to {b} to {c}.

## Implications of this plan

This is worth mentioning here:

Group {a} may feel left out, may not feel involved. They will misunderstand your concept of discipleship.

Group {b} could be reached too quickly. Their "assistance" or even "support" must not be misinterpreted as commitment.

Group {c} need a definite time, place and schedule for discipling. It is these people who will be your right hand in evangelism and outreach. They are your FAT people "Faithful", "Available" and "Teachable".

# 4. PRACTICAL SUGGESTIONS.

## 4:1 Witnessing:

AIM—To train each disciple to be an active witness. This would help them to know how to lead someone else to Christ. They will need to articulate the Gospel, to recognize the importance of follow-up and discipleship, and to know what it means to "multiply".

Start small, not big. Start with small group activities. The work must be carefully      monitored.

Witnessing should be a way of life, not just through the church program.

Prayer, a burden for the lost, and the filling of the Holy Spirit, are all vital ingredients.

## 4:2 Church services:

Give careful attention to:

- Content of the preaching—relevancy—doctrine.
- The style of the service to be person-orientated.
- Good preparation of the music.
- Ministry to the various groups present.
- Welcoming of all at the door and especially the visitors.
- Counselors always to be available.

Prayer strategy for the whole service,—this is not even an option.

## 4:3 Outreaches:

- Crusade—Mission—appropriate time, relevant and well organized, advertising, etc of the best class.
- Guest services, seeker-friendly services, involving the total congregation and geared to the outsider.
- Men's breakfasts.
- Ladies' coffee mornings.
- Newspaper evangelism.
- Literature drops, i.e strategic places determined before time. This needs to be well presented, containing a clear Gospel message.
- Child evangelism. Never underestimate the value of a child.

## 4:4 Follow-up.

Some important points to be remembered :

- A register to be kept of every commitment made in the life of the church.
- A follow-up letter to go to the person who makes a commitment.
- Enroll new converts in a Bible study group in their area.
- Assign spiritual parents for every spiritual baby born.
- Accountability. Develop a spread sheet on which details of what is done for every new convert are recorded.

- Seek to go the full circle: "evangelism is never completed until the evangelized begin to evangelize"

- Emphasize the spiritual dimension. If this is neglected, the "how" becomes superfluous.

- Remember and honor the work of the Holy Spirit.

- Bathe every matter in prayer.

- Faith versus risk is a great challenge.

- Remember "very often you lose them." Very often, once you have trained them, you actually lose them as they are called elsewhere. They are busy spreading the Gospel abroad.

Because of the "what" and "why", the "how" becomes the most exciting aspect of the Main Thing.

# Conclusion

As we conclude this book with its emphasis on the "Main Thing", I thought it would be an encouragement to share a number of stories concerning the Grace of God.

One of the most beautiful stories I have heard and shared with many, many people, is the story of "The Little Man with White Hair in Sydney, Australia." To keep the story as accurate as possible, I am quoting from an Evangelical Conference in Sydney, 1987, when one Charles McLeod challenged individuals as to their response. His theme was "P.O.R.—Press On Regardless." He shared instances given by Rev. Francis Dixon of the Lansdowne Baptist Church, Bournemouth, England, as follows:

> During a testimony meeting in his church, a young man called Peter stood up and said , " I was walking down George Street in Sydney one Sunday night when, out of nowhere it seemed, a man came and spoke courteously to me; "I would like to say a few words to you and I hope you won't be offended. Do you know where you are going to live in eternity—heaven or hell? It's a very important matter. That is all. Good-night, sir."
> I thought over this very much, and when I returned to England, I found a Christian who helped me. It was that man in George Street who started me on my way to Christ." A few weeks later Mr. Dixon arranged for a Mission Team to visit his church, and a young man by the name of Noel gave his testimony. He said, "I was stationed in Sydney in the armed forces, and one Sunday night while walking

down George Street, a man came out of the dim light and said to me, "Excuse me, sir, I have a very important matter to share with you. I hope you won't be offended, and I won't keep you long. Do you know where you are going to spend eternity—heaven or hell? It is very serious, sir. Good-night!" It was that man's word which helped me to know that I really needed Christ.

After the meeting, Peter said to Noel, "You know, you have my testimony!" And they wondered who that man would be.

Shortly after this Francis Dixon made his first visit to Australia, to interest folks in the Lansdowne Bible School and Postal Fellowship.

Preaching in an Adelaide Baptist Church, he spoke about Peter and Noel and the man, and a man interrupted his message and said , "Can I give my testimony?" "By all means", said Francis Dixon. The man said, "I was walking down George Street, Sydney, on Sunday night, when out of nowhere came this man who spoke to me like he did to Peter and Noel, and was the means of my conversion."

Later, preaching in a Baptist Church in Perth, West Australia, being so impressed about Peter, Noel and the Adelaide man, he included this in his sermon. After the service a deacon came to him and said, "That too is my testimony." On his return to England, and reporting on his visit to Australia, he mentioned the men from Adelaide and Perth, along with Peter and Noel. After the service an amazing thing happened. A woman came to him and said, "I was stationed in the military forces in Sydney, when one Sunday night in George Street, a man courteously spoke to me as mentioned previously, and this was the means of leading me to Christ."

Being invited to speak at the Keswick Deeper Life Convention, Francis Dixon, in his address, mentioned the wonderful sequence of events concerning the man who spoke about eternity, in George Street, Sydney. Following the meeting, a man came up to him and said, "I am another one." Francis Dixon visited India to speak at a Missionary Conference, after which one of the older missionaries came up to him and said, "I am another one."

Later he went to Jamaica and told them of the Indian missionary, the woman from his own church, as well as the five other people. At the end of the service another man approached Mr Dixon and said, 'I was in Sydney, when out of nowhere came this man who said, "I hope I won't offend you, but I have something very important to say: after you pass from this world where will you spend eternity—in heaven or hell? That is all, good-night. God bless you.' " Who, Mr. Dixon wondered, was the unknown man who spoke of "eternity".

Later he made another visit to Sydney, and speaking to the late Al Gilchrist, he said, "Would you by any chance know of a man who spoke to the people personally about eternity, in George Street?" "Yes", said Alec "I know him. His name is Frank Genner, although he is too old and too ill for much today. He lives in an outer Sydney suburb, and I can take you to him." He took Francis Dixon to a small homely cottage, where he was introduced to the unknown man who spoke of "eternity". When Francis Dixon told him of the eight people who had spoken about him, but did not know him, tears came into his eyes and he said, "I don't know how many thousands of times I have walked up and down George Street and spoken to people personally about "eternity" but this is the first time I've ever heard of anyone really coming to Christ for eternal life."

To me, that is the most striking part of the entire story. Although he witnessed to many, he didn't how many, if any, had come to Christ.

I was in Australia two years ago and made enquiries about "The Little Man with White Hair." After some enquiries, I met a friend who said they knew all about him; in fact his daughter was a member of their church. Her name was Ann. Through a number of events, I was able to meet his daughter Ann on the phone and asked questions about her Dad. She told me what a great man of God he was. On a Saturday after-noon at 4 o'clock, he always shined his shoes to get ready to meet the King of Kings the next day. It was esti-mated that in the lifetime of Frank Genner, there were approximately 250, 000 who professed faith in Christ, directly or indirectly, as a result of his witnessing. I walked down George Street in Sydney. I asked another friend where he thought he might have stood. He said possibly outside the Post Office. I remember walking up and down outside the Post Office and saying to myself "Oh God, make me a witness". I was able to witness in some of the areas around there.

While in Sydney, waiting for my friend to meet me for lunch, I went into a shop and was browsing around when a shop assistant asked if he could help me. I said I was just looking around and waiting for a friend. He then said, "Oh, I recognize that accent". I said, "Really, where do you think I am from?" He said, "South Africa". I said, "How did you know?", to which he replied, "Oh, we have many South Africans coming here. In fact we just had the South African rugby team in our shop." He then went on to describe one of the players who had spoken to him for a long time, and was a very pleasant person. "In fact, he said he was a Born Again Christian," said the shop assistant. I said, "Born Again; what does that mean?"

He replied "Oh, his whole life has been changed, and he lives daily for the Lord." He described the man to me. I mentioned his name, and said, "yes, I believe he is a Christian," then turned to him and said, "are you a Christian?" He said, "Oh, no." Then he said "What about you, sir?"

I said, "Yes, I am." He then made the following statement, "I've only had a serious chat with two South Africans in my life, and you have both challenged me about the fact of eternal life. Maybe now is the time to consider this."

I said to him, "Sir, do you know why I am standing here?", to which he replied, "No." I said, "God has brought me here to help you clinch this deal about receiving Christ as your Saviour." He then went on to describe the churches with whom he had had connections, the disappointments and so on, but indicated a real interest. I said, "You know we can pray right here and you can receive Christ."

He said, "Oh no, I would be fired for praying while on the job." I said to him, "I'm not here for long, but I can meet you afterwards, or could I arrange for a friend to meet you?" He agreed to this, and since then, I have heard of the regular association my friend has had with him, and that he has been attending a Bible Study. I cannot tell you that he has made a real commitment, but there has been an interest, and he asked for my card, which has a prayer on it whereby he could pray to receive Christ. When I returned home, I sent a message to the sports player, and he was thrilled that just a mere witness in a shop in downtown Sydney, had resulted in this connection .

You see, we can be witnesses anywhere.

I remember being up in Bulawayo, Zimbabwe, waiting at an hotel for a conference to start. I'd met with our Malawian representative and after dinner we were sitting in the living room of the hotel when a little fellow about ten years of age, came and sat opposite us. He started asking questions. I asked him what he was doing, and he told me that he and his family were about to leave to go back to England and they were spending a few days at the hotel. He proceeded to tell me a number of things he knew about the hotel, which would not be suitable to put down in print.

He then turned and said, "And where are you from?" I said, "South Africa." He said, "Oh, you must be a big businessman." I said, "No, but I am in big business." To which he replied, "Well, what is your business." I said, "I am in the business of getting people to heaven." He said, "Well, how do you get them to heaven?" I said, " How do you think I get them to heaven?" He said, "I suppose you kill them first!" To which I replied, "No, I don't, but you know you can be sure." He said, "I don't know." I then proceeded to explain the way of salvation, and I said, "You can pray right now and receive the gift." He said, "Oh no, everybody is watching. I couldn't do it." I then said, "I have a card here with a prayer on it." He said, "Could I have it?'

I said, "Yes." He said, "I tell you what, I will take it home tonight, and I will pray that prayer, and let you know."

The conference started the next day and I never saw the little fellow again. However, he saw the Malawian, and this was the message I had from him: "Tell that South African I prayed the prayer, and if I never see him again, I will see him in heaven!"

We can be witnesses wherever we are. Sometimes when I'm on an airplane, instead of saying I am a minister of the Gospel, I will find out what work they are doing. For instance, if they say they are in personnel work, I will say as a matter of interest I'm also in personnel. I work amongst people, developing them in their skills, so that they can know the Greatest Person on earth and in heaven—the Lord Jesus.

If a man says he is an electrician, I say that's strange, I'm also an electrician. I help people to light up their lives!

I once sat next to a man who told me he was a book-keeper and an accountant. I said that was interesting because I'm also an accountant. I then explained that I would have to give an account of him one day before God. I once spoke to a lady from America in one of our Game Parks She was an educationist and asked if I was also in the tourist business. I explained that I was also in the tourist business, and that in fact, I lead tours all around the world, and even further. To which she said ,"Where?". I said, "Well I take tours to heaven!" She laughed at me, and said, "Of course I don't believe in that; in fact I'm an atheist." I then showed her the futility of being an atheist, and concluded our discussion by saying, "If I am wrong and get to the end of the road, and have made a mistake, I have lost nothing. But if you are wrong, and you get to the end of the road, you're in trouble!" She had to acknowledge and concede it was a point.

I don't intend to use this as boasting by any means, but simply to say, use any opportunity, and God will use you to be a witness for Him. After all that is what we are called to do.

I want you to prayerfully consider this poem from an anonymous writer :

My friend, I stand in judgement now;
and feel that you're to blame somehow;

On earth I walked with you day by day
And never did you point the way,

You know the Lord in Truth and Glory
But never did you tell the story.

My knowledge then was very dim,
You could have led me safe to Him,

Though we lived together on the earth
You never told me of the second birth.

And now I stand this day condemned,
Because you failed to mention Him.

You taught me many things, that's true
I called you 'friend' and trusted you;

But I learn now that it's too late;
You could have kept me from this fate.

We walked by day and talked by night,
And yet you showed me not the light.

You let me live and love and die;
You knew I'd never live on high.
Yes, I called you friend in life
And trusted you through joy and strife.

And yet, on coming to this end;
I cannot now call you 'my friend'.

# Endnotes

1. Chapter 2 page 5—*Hitler's Cross* by Erwin Lutzer—Publisher Moody Press

2. Chapter 2 page 9—*The Gates of Hell Shall Not Prevail* by Dr James Kennedy Publisher Nelson

3. Chapter 3 page 5—*Master Plan of Evangelism* by Dr Robert Coleman—Publisher Revell